Ink, Blood, and Prayer

Kiera J. Gerety

Copyright © 2025 by Kiera J. Gerety and Bluebonnet Books, LLC.

All rights reserved.

ISBN: 979-8-9929704-2-5

No part of this publication may be reproduced, distributed, or transmitted in any form or by any means, including photocopying, recording, or other electronic or mechanical methods, without the prior written permission of the publisher, except as permitted by U.S. copyright law. For permission requests, contact bluebonnetbookspublishing@gmail.com.

For privacy reasons, some names, locations, and dates may have been changed.

Book Cover Design by Daniel de la Fe

Edited by Chelsea Schermerhorn

First edition 2025

From the Author:

This book is raw. It does not soften the edges of survival, addiction, trauma, or recovery; however, there is hope after addiction. Please take care of yourself as you read, and know that it is okay to step away if something becomes too much.

Major Themes & Content Warnings:

- Substance Use & Addiction – References to drug use (heroin, cocaine, alcohol), relapse, cravings, withdrawal, and the emotional weight of addiction.
- Self-Harm & Suicidal Ideation – Descriptions of self-inflicted injuries, scars, thoughts of ending one's life, and the struggle to keep going.
- Emotional Neglect & Psychological Abuse – Experiences of being dismissed, invalidated, or made to feel unworthy in relationships.
- Trauma & PTSD – Flashbacks, intrusive thoughts, and the lasting impact of past pain.
- Shame & Self-Loathing – Internalized feelings of worthlessness, societal judgment, and struggles with self-acceptance.
- Grief & Loss – Mourning people, past versions of oneself, and opportunities that will never return.
- Mental Health Struggles – Depression, anxiety, dissociation, and the difficulty of navigating daily life while carrying heavy emotional burdens.
- Medical & Bureaucratic Neglect – The frustration of being dismissed by healthcare systems, struggling with affordability, and being told survival is a privilege, not a right.
- Witchcraft, Spirituality & Energy Work – References to tarot, protection magic, Reiki, ancestral work, and ritual cleansing in the context of healing.

For Readers Who Need It:

You don't have to read this all at once. You don't have to read every page. If something is too much, it's okay to set it down and return when you're ready—or not at all. If you need grounding, take a deep breath, drink some water, hold something solid in your hands. You are here. You are real. You are not alone.

If you are in crisis, please reach out to someone. There is no shame in needing help. You are worth saving.

Take care of yourself as you move through these words. You deserve gentleness and recognition for the strength it takes to face them.

Allison, this wouldn't be possible without you.
I wouldn't be alive to write this without you.

Foreword

I didn't write this book to be pretty. I didn't write it to be inspiring, or palatable, or easy to swallow. I wrote it because I had to—because the weight of it sat too long in my chest, pressing down on my ribs, choking out the breath I needed to keep going. I wrote it because there are things I could never say out loud, things I tried to bury beneath the years, beneath sobriety, beneath the quiet lie that healing means forgetting.

But forgetting has never been my way.

This book is a record, a reckoning, a bloodletting. It is every moment I thought I wouldn't make it, and every time I did. It is the ache that still lingers in my bones, the scars that still catch the light, the names I still whisper when I see certain cars on the street. It is the weight of shame, of relapse, of loneliness so thick it wraps around you like a second skin. It is the blade, the bottle, the needle, the silence. It is the ghosts I carried for years, the ones I am still learning how to set down.

This is not a book about getting better. This is a book about getting through—the relentless, unpolished reality of survival, of facing each day despite the weight of it all. It is about healing in fragments, about endurance when there are no easy answers.

If I have learned anything, it is this: pain does not disappear just because we choose to heal. It shifts, it transforms, it weaves itself into the fabric of who we are. It does not let go, but we can learn to hold it differently. Not as a burden, not as a brand, but as a testament that we are still here.

And if you are reading this, then you are still here too.

That is enough. That has always been enough.

As my wife once told me "I'm not scared of you spreading your wings. I'm scared of you cutting them off."

Kiera J Gerety

February 2025

Contents

From the Author: 3
Foreword 6
I. Fire and Ash 9
    Ashes in the Veins 10
    The Brown Tar's Curse 11
    Sweet Death 12
    The Shadow's Embrace 13
    War Inside 14
    Shards of Grace 16
    Red, White, and Brown 18
II. Scarred but Standing 19
    Fine Print 20
    Snowbound 21
    A Tattered Edge 22
III. The Road Back 23
    What Remains, What Grows 24
    Ash and Air 25
    Kia Soul 27
    One Day, Maybe 28
    One More Fucking Sip, One More Fucking Breath 29
    The Loneliest Seat in the House 31
IV. Where the Ash Settles 32
    The Noise That Comes After 33
    The Long Way Back 34
    Letters to the Ones I Lost 36
V. Between Ruin and Revelation 38
    The Second First Time 39
    Scales Fell Like Rain 41
    When the Gods Found Me 43
    The Weight of Me 45
    Between Hoofbeats and Whispers 47
    The Way Home 48
    This Time, I Breathe 49
    Muted, Unmuted, Still Here 50
    Fire, Earth, and Breath 51
VI. Waking the Bones 53
    Between Hoofbeats and Currents 54
    The Hex Unwoven 55
    Between Light and Shadow 56
    Hekate's Crossroads 57
    By Silver Thread and Spindle's Weave 58
    Forge My Fury 59
    Hallowed Ground 60
VII. In Closing 61
    The Cold Unknown 62
    Longing for the Forest 63
    A Garland of Blossoms 64

I. Fire and Ash
Between the High and the Hollow

Addiction is not just the act of using. It is the hunger, the waiting, the fight that never really ends. It is the war between the part of you that wants to live and the part that only knows how to self-destruct. It does not leave clean scars. It lingers, pressing into the bones, whispering in quiet moments, aching beneath the surface even when you've sworn you've left it behind.

This section explores the wreckage addiction leaves in its wake—the burned bridges, the shattered bodies, the nights spent staring at the ceiling, too exhausted to fight but too angry to let go. It reveals how addiction tempts, how it promises stillness and relief, and how it lies. It is about craving something you know will kill you and wanting it anyway.

This section is also about the war of staying clean—not the polished, smiling version, but the raw, teeth-grinding reality of it. The battle that happens when no one is watching, when the world expects you to be "better," but the sickness still lingers beneath the surface. The shame of relapse. The exhaustion of starting over. The unbearable weight of knowing that sobriety does not erase the past, nor does it silence the voice that tells you one more hit, one more drink, one more escape will be enough.

This is not a story of easy redemption. It is a story of survival—of standing still while the fire rages, while the shadows press in, while the past drags its nails down your spine and begs you to come back. It is about choosing, moment-by-moment, breath-by-breath, to stay. To fight. To endure.

Ashes in the Veins

Under the yellow glare of the streetlight's hum,
Where rats feast and broken men come,
I found the devil in powdered white—
A quick escape, a hollow flight.
It burned my throat, it froze my tongue,
It brought me nothing but a song unsung.
I was a queen with a paper crown,
Doomed to crumble, crashing down.

The grind was endless, the hunger raw,
Hands outstretched, a scraping claw.
Money from my fingers slipped
Each hit a toll from my soul ripped.
I knew the taste of wintered nights,
Of gnawing cold and alley fights.
The dust it called, it dragged, it clung,
A bitter hymn my body sung.

But there, beneath a flickering sign,
I stumbled in, past borrowed time.
The air was stale, the light was dim,
And every face looked worn and grim.
Their words were sharp as shattered glass,
Each truth a scar, each pain a past.
I sat in silence, numb and spent,
While shame poured out in each lament.

"My name is..."—Gods, I couldn't speak,
My voice was dry, my spirit weak.
But they just nodded, eyes like mine,
Like echoes caught in a twisted line.
Their stories cut, their anger bled,
And in the storm, I saw what led
To hope's return, to one last fight—
The slow crawl out, toward the light.

Now, the devil's there, but chained up tight,
His whisper distant, teeth out of sight.
The streets still stink, the grind's still rough,
But there's a spark, and it's enough.
The dust is gone, the hunger fades,
The nights aren't traps; they're passing shades.
And though the dark still calls my name,
I walk with others, scarred the same.

The Brown Tar's Curse

Beneath a sickly, fading moon,
where shadows twist and silence lingers,
I walked a road of endless gray,
led by whispers soft as smoke.
The tar's deep voice, sweet and low,
A fire's glow, promised warmth.
But what it gave, it stole in kind—
a hollow mind, a prick of the pin.

I once held gold in my hands,
watched it slip like water through my fingers.
The taverns, back alleys, the nameless doors—
they became my world, my waking dream.
Pocket-empty, soul stripped bare,
I chased the numbness into the dark
That chained me down,
until dawn reached out with frail hands.

On that night heavy with loss,
a voice called through the noise.
"Come inside. Share your story.
The road is long, but you don't walk it alone."

A circle, a room, a place to breathe—
where hands didn't turn me away,
where eyes held something long forgotten.
Through shaking lips, I let truth spill,
poured out like the last drops in a broken bottle.

No judgment, no shame—only nods,
only voices that knew the same weight,
only hands steady enough to hold what I couldn't.

Now, where the tar once settled in my veins,
something else has taken root.

The sky isn't ashen anymore.
The curse is broken.
I walk the road still, but not alone.
Storms may rise, the past may call,
but I stand beneath a different sky.
And this time, I stay.
...for now.

Sweet Death

Ice drips through my veins,
Coursing with unrelenting pain,
As I wait—aching—for sweet relief.
The needle pierces deep,
The chamber swells,
The plunger whispers its fatal spell.
I close my eyes,
Unbind the ties.
Breath falters, hollow and slow,
Following the shadows
Of those who've come before,
Knocking softly on this final door.
My eyes snap shut—
Is this my cruel lot?
Death clings to the rig,
A life reduced to dregs.

The Shadow's Embrace

Loneliness settles deep, a slow-burning ember,
pressing into the places I swore I'd forget.
The needle called my name in the hush of night,
a fleeting heat, a stolen moment—
warm as summer air, gone just as fast,
leaving only an empty road behind.

At the edge of another lost evening,
bottles scatter at my feet,
the sky above me a hollow void.
Relief whispers from the bottom of a glass,
its promise as bitter as the burn in my throat.

I drink anyway—anything to silence the noise.
A line of white, a trail of surrender,
sliding fast through my veins.
The world softens, blurs at the edges,
shadows stirring in places I swore were locked.

Memories claw their way forward—
faces I buried, words I never spoke.
Each sip, each hit, another thread in the web,
pulling tight around my ribs.

The past lingers like smoke,
wrapping around the choices I can't undo,
the dreams I left behind,
the nights I swore would be the last.

But somewhere beyond the wreckage,
a whisper cuts through the haze.
A voice I almost remember—
one that speaks of something else,
something softer, something real.

Maybe one day I'll find a way out.
Maybe one day I'll let the light in.
But tonight, the shadow holds me close,
its grip heavy, its silence familiar.
Still, I hum a song too quiet to name,
a prayer for the day I rise again.

War Inside

Four days clean,
but my body remembers.
The ache sits in my chest,
a hungry thing,
a snarling thing,
a beast with my name
tattooed on its teeth.

I sit with it,
hands gripping the edge of the sink,
knuckles white,
staring into the mirror
like it owes me an answer.
But it just stares back—
the same eyes,
the same hollow hunger.

I can still feel the line,
burning sharp and fast,
the rail of powder pulling me
into a bright, humming nothing.
I can feel it even now—
a ghost slithering up my nose,
a phantom rushing my blood.
I want it.
God, I want it.
More than sleep,
more than food,
more than the quiet life
I swore I'd fight for.

Four days clean,
and it's a goddamn war.
The phone stares at me,
a coiled snake.
I could call,
I could text,
I could find what I need
in fifteen minutes flat.
But instead, I grit my teeth,
dig nails into my palm,
and let the beast scream.

This isn't bravery.
This isn't victory.
It's just standing still

while the fire burns around me,
while my own brain
scratches at the walls of my skull,
howling for one more hit,
one more line,
one more escape.

Four days clean,
and I hate myself for wanting it.
I hate myself for stopping.
But I hate the person I was
even more.
So I stay here,
letting the hunger claw,
letting the beast gnash its teeth.
Four days,
and maybe tomorrow
I'll make it five.

Shards of Grace

Five years clean, I wore it proud,
A warrior's strength beneath the shroud.
The echoes of pipes, of powders, of shame,
Sealed in a vault, a forgotten name.
I held my head high, my path was straight,
A beacon burning against my fate.
But grace is brittle, a fragile thread,
And old temptations are never dead.

The doctor's voice was warm and kind,
"A helper for your busy mind.
Focus sharp, the edge you crave,
Just one small pill, and you'll be saved."
I nodded, smiling, feeling strong,
What harm in aid to move along?
But one became two, then three, then more,
And the hunger knocked on my soul's door.

Days ran dry; nights burned bright,
Eyes wide open, no end in sight.
A thousand thoughts, a racing heart,
The old fire flared, tore me apart.
I told myself it wasn't the same—
This wasn't the needle, the bitter game.
But in the mirror, her face I knew,
The ghost I'd buried came breaking through.

Eighteen months of spinning lies,
Of shadows creeping, bloodshot eyes.
The pills grew scarce, the walls closed tight,
The weight of truth too sharp, too right.
I hit the floor, a hollow shell,
A prisoner chained in a private hell.
I screamed to the dark, a desperate call,
Not for death, but a chance to fall—
Into arms that wouldn't let me drown,
Into grace that wouldn't cut me down.

Back to the circle, the faces worn,
Where shame meets hope, where lives are torn.
I stood among them, voice a quiver,
Each word a blade, each truth a sliver.
"I fell again," I said through tears,
"I drowned in whispers, in old fears."
They didn't flinch, they didn't jeer,
Their hands reached out, their voices clear:

"We've been there too; we know the pain.
Together we rise, again and again."

Clean once more, but scarred and bruised,
A life rebuilt, the past refused.
The ghost of pills still whispers low,
A tempting siren I've come to know.
But I walk this road, my sisters near,
Their strength my shield, their grace sincere.
Through shadow's pull, I find my way,
One step, one breath, one honest day.

Red, White, and Brown

Twelve weeks clean, and I should feel proud.
That's what they tell me.
That's what I tell myself.
But pride doesn't quiet the shaking,
doesn't fill the hollow ache in my ribs,
doesn't stop the itch buried deep in my skin.
The cravings don't hit all at once—
they creep in slow, like water rising,
seeping through the cracks I swore I'd sealed.
A whisper at first, then a scream:
Just one. Just a taste. Just enough.
I press the blade to my thigh,
watch the red rise to the surface,
the only relief I'm allowed.
It doesn't burn like the rush,
doesn't hush my thoughts like a line up my nose,
doesn't steal my breath the way
heroin did,
cooked down, drawn up,
sliding through my veins like a promise.
I don't miss the sickness,
the withdrawal that gnawed my bones raw.
I don't miss waking up on piss-stained floors,
sweating out the ghosts of the night before.
But I miss the silence.
I miss the stillness after the hit,
the weightlessness before the crash.
I run my fingers over the scars on my legs,
crosshatched maps of every time I said no
and nearly meant it.
I know the feeling will pass.
I know I'll make it to thirteen weeks,
fourteen, maybe more.
But tonight, I sit with it.
The wanting, the war.
The blade in one hand, my phone in the other.
Sponsor's number memorized.
My name known in the rooms of recovery.
I won't use.
I don't think I will.
But fuck, I want to.
And that's the part no one wants to talk about.

II. Scarred but Standing
What Remains After the Fire

This section is not about being healed. It is about the days you wake up and the war hasn't ended, but you get up anyway. It is about the moments when your mind tells you to disappear, to give in, to fold under the weight of it all—and yet, somehow, you stay.

Scarred but Standing is about the kind of survival that isn't gentle or poetic. It is the survival that looks like dragging yourself through another day when your bones feel too heavy to carry. It is learning to live in a body that still flinches from old wounds, a mind that still echoes with ghosts that refuse to leave. It is about knowing the darkness so well it has become familiar, but choosing, even in the smallest way, to reach for something beyond it.

There is no pretending here. No pretending that systems built to help don't sometimes fail, that healing is a straight path, that recovery is anything but a relentless, brutal fight. No pretending that some days, staying alive feels more like defiance than triumph. But there is something in the defiance. Something in the standing, even when you shake.

This section is for the ones still gripping the edge, still fighting to believe in a life beyond the wreckage. The ones who have been to the depths and still carry the weight of it in their bones. The ones who are still here, even when it would have been easier not to be.

You are scarred. You are still standing. That is enough. That has always been enough.

Fine Print

I tell myself, today will be the day,
whisper it like a prayer, like a promise,
but my hands are cowards, and my ribs still rise,
lungs like rusted bellows, stalling, stalling.
It isn't fair to wake up in a body not my own,
stitched together by pills that promised salvation
but only carved me into something heavier,
something harder to carry.
The ones who count dollars instead of lives
wrote my sentence in fine print,
let me read it over and over,
trapped in the margins of policies and denials.
They say I am worth only what I can pay.
They say suffering is a deductible expense.
They say my survival is negotiable,
so long as I have the right coverage.
And yet:
Here I am.
I don't know why.
I don't have an answer that makes sense.
Maybe I am just too tired to be brave,
or too stubborn to let them win.
But for now—
I stay.

Snowbound

The urge claws deep, a beast untamed,
Its voice a whisper, sharp, unashamed.
The blade calls softly, promises peace,
A fleeting silence, a false release.

But I won't give in—I can't, not tonight.
I fling myself into winter's bite.
The snow's raw sting, a bitter reprieve,
A cold distraction I'm forced to believe.

Breath clouds the air, sharp and thin,
I let the frost bite deeper than skin.
Each flake that melts against my face
Reminds me there's still something to chase.

The ache doesn't leave; it clings like a ghost,
A shadow lingering where I need it most.
But here in the snow, I fight, and I stay,
Hoping this chill will keep harm away.

Because somewhere beneath this numbing frost,
Is a part of me worth more than I've lost.
So I'll freeze before I break, enduring the cold,
Fighting for a story yet to be told.

A Tattered Edge

The blade whispers secrets, soft as rain,
Etching silence into lines of pain.
Each stroke, a sentence, raw, unplanned,
A dialogue spoken through trembling hands.
The mirror, my enemy, reflects too clear,
The hollowed eyes that house the fear.

But pain is a tether, a muted plea,
A language carved that no one can see.
The blood beads bright, a fleeting bloom,
Petals of red in a sterile room.
It pools, then fades, a vanishing trace,
Like whispers lost without a face.

What is release but a fleeting breath,
A dance on the edge of life and death?
The sting, the hush, the moment's grace—
A brief escape, a soft embrace.

Yet no blade has ever held me close,
No wound has ever answered back.
The ache remains when steel runs cold,
The silence deeper, the night intact.

Still, beneath the storm, a flicker glows,
A seed of strength in the shadowed throes.
Though rough the path, though steep the climb,
The heart beats on, defying time.

III. The Road Back
No Straight Lines, No Easy Roads

Healing isn't a straight line. It isn't a clean break from the past or a sudden realization that makes everything easier. It's slow, messy, and full of days that feel like nothing has changed at all. The Road Back isn't about being "fixed." It's about learning how to keep going, even when the past still lingers, even when the cravings don't disappear, even when you don't know if you believe in the future yet.

The weight of old wounds doesn't just vanish. Some days, it presses in harder than others—triggered by a song, a voice, the wrong car on the wrong street. The past stays, but it doesn't hold all the power anymore. It becomes something you carry, something that shaped you but doesn't get to define you.

There are no grand breakthroughs here, no promises that everything suddenly gets easier. Some days, it's just about making it through without slipping, about keeping the ghosts at a distance long enough to breathe. It's the small things that hold you together—a cup of coffee in the morning, the weight of a stone in your palm, the simple act of waking up and deciding, however reluctantly, to keep going.

It's not about being healed. It's about staying. It's about standing up, even when your legs shake. It's about learning, little by little, how to live with what remains without letting it drown you. And that's enough. Some days, that's everything.

What Remains, What Grows

The past does not leave quietly.
It lingers like the scent of old sweat in thrift store clothes,
like blood rusted into the weave of a bedsheet,
like the burn of whiskey long after the bottle is empty.
I trace my scars, mapping out the history of every fight,
every night spent pressed against a bathroom floor,
the sting of a belt, the sharp kiss of metal,
the places where I tried to carve myself into something softer,
something easier to hold.
Some wounds never close right.
They stay tender at the edges,
aching when the weather turns,
when a certain song plays,
when a voice from another room sounds too much like his.
But I am still here.
And so is the wreckage,
but it no longer owns me.
The guilt is still there,
but it does not break my ribs when I breathe.
The grief still comes knocking,
but I no longer set a place for it at the table.
I am learning how to hold the past without letting it drown me,
how to touch the scars without reopening them.
I have seen trees grow around barbed wire,
the rust buried deep in the bark,
not gone, but no longer stopping the bloom.

Ash and Air

She kills the engine
but leaves the heat on.
Outside, the trees rattle,
bare-boned in the wind.
Inside, just us.
The car smells like stale coffee,
nicotine, regret.
Her coat slumps over the console.
Her hands rest easy on the wheel.
Like we're just two women
killing time on a back road
where no one can hear.
"Whenever you're ready."
But how the fuck
could I ever be ready?
How do you pull something
out of your throat
without choking on it?
Without the world shifting,
her fingers tightening on the keys,
her eyes landing on me,
seeing what I already know—
that I am a thing to leave behind.
I press my nails into my palm.
Half-moons rise in my skin.
I stare at the dashboard dust,
cracked leather,
fog curling against glass.
And then, I just say it.
The words come out like something
pried loose from my ribs,
like a tooth rotten to the root,
a wound too deep to sew shut.
Silence.
I brace for it.
For the look. For the shift.
For the weight of my own filth
settling between us.
But she doesn't move.
Doesn't flinch.
Just lights a cigarette,
cracks the window,
exhales slow,
like we've got all the time in the world.
"Most kids go through those phases."
The weight changes.

Not gone. Not forgotten.
But it doesn't press so hard anymore.
It's out. It exists.
Maybe she'll never understand.
Maybe no one ever will.
But I said it.
The wind pushes through the trees,
branches groaning, something breaking loose.
I roll my window down,
breathe in the cold.
For the first time in forever,
I can finally breathe.
A fourth step finally complete—
seven years later.

Kia Soul

We met in the places where young people in recovery
go to forget how close they once came to dying—
game nights, bonfires, road trips with the windows down,
laughing too loud at things only we could understand.
We were the ones who made it.
We were supposed to be lucky.
Jon never said much, but he didn't have to.
He carried himself like someone who had already won,
like the past was a story he'd closed the book on.
Me? I still felt like I was dragging it behind me,
like a rope tied too tight around my ribs.
Like no matter how many meetings I sat through,
no matter how many days I marked clean,
I was still one step away from the edge.
Maybe he saw it too.
The way I clung to something I couldn't name.
The way my hands shook when I counted tips at the end of a shift.
The way I drank Monster like it could fill the space
where heroin used to live.
"Still a waitress?"
His voice was always too careful, too light,
like he was trying to make it sound like small talk.
Like he wasn't ashamed of me.
Like I didn't feel that shame
burning through my skin every time he asked.
Now, it's the green Kia Soul that does it.
Doesn't matter who's driving—
every time I see one,
I'm 25 again, standing outside his car,
his voice even, detached, measured.
"I just think you have more potential than this."
I don't know where he is now.
Probably still stacking years like poker chips,
probably never thinking of me.
But I am still here.
Still standing. Still waking up.
Still making it through one day, then the next.
Still trying to find a way
to let go of the weight
without letting go of myself.

One Day, Maybe

I sit in another meeting,
folding the words into my lap like a worn-out prayer.
"Just for today."
"It gets better."
"Keep coming back."
I say them like I believe them.
Like they aren't heavy in my mouth,
like they don't taste like dust and old ghosts.
The past still lingers in strange places.
A song in the grocery store knocks the wind out of me.
A street I used to haunt makes my hands shake on the wheel.
I dream of people I swore I'd forget,
wake up with their names pressed into my ribs.
My body still remembers before my mind does.
Before I can brace myself, I am back—
on the floor, in the cold, in the silence of another bad night.
I tell myself I am not there anymore.
I tell myself I am here, I am clean,
I am doing everything right.
But some days, I still wonder if I'll ever be whole again.
If the missing pieces will always ache like phantom limbs.
If I'll ever stop reaching for something that is gone.
I trace the ink on my wrist,
"Let go, let God."
Run my thumb over the letters,
as if they could sink in deeper,
as if I could etch them into my bones.
Some days, they feel like a lifeline.
Some days, they feel like a lie.
But I wake up.
I drink my coffee.
I show up for work.
I sit in the meeting.
I listen to the same stories, the same voices,
watch the same lost kids stumble in from the rain.
I tell them to stay.
I tell them to hold on.
Like I believe it.
And maybe, one day, I will.
Maybe one day the weight will lift.
Maybe one day the past will let me go.
Maybe not today. Maybe not tomorrow.
But I'll stay long enough to find out.

One More Fucking Sip, One More Fucking Breath

Wake up.
Not because I want to,
but because I said I would.
Because the sun still rises,
and my name still belongs in this world,
even if some days I wish it didn't.

I light a candle,
watch the flame flicker,
hold my hands above it,
let the heat bite my skin—
not enough to hurt, just enough to feel.

It's not the same as the rush,
but it's something.

I make a café mocha from the Keurig,
watch the swirl of chocolate and coffee
blend into something smooth,
something almost comforting.
I breathe in the steam,
let it coat my throat,
drink slow,
like I have all the time in the world,
like this is enough.

I press my feet into the earth,
let the dirt hold me steady.
Cold grass, wet ground,
the weight of my own body.
This is where I am now.
This is where I stay.

The cravings come in the quiet.
Not loud, not sudden,
just a whisper in my ribs,
a hand on my shoulder,
a ghost saying,
"Wouldn't it be easier?"
And fuck, maybe it would.
Maybe I could chase the numbness,
crash my way back into oblivion,
throw away every goddamn thing I fought for.
Maybe I could.
But I don't.
Not today.

Instead, I run cold water over my wrists,
feel the pulse beneath my skin,
proof that I am still here.

I clutch a stone,
rub my thumb against its rough edges,
ground myself in something solid,
something real.

I whisper my name,
like an incantation,
like a spell,
like a promise.

And I stay.
Again.
And again.
And again.

The Loneliest Seat in the House

The ballroom hums with voices, thousands packed in shoulder to shoulder,
but the space inside me is cavernous, hollow.
Laughter rings out, warm and easy,
people pulling each other into hugs, clasping hands,
a shared language of belonging I never quite learned.
I sit in the back, sipping burnt coffee from a paper cup,
watching the tide of conversation move without me.

Someone at the mic shares their story—
the kind that should tether me to this moment,
the kind that should remind me why I'm here.

Instead, their words drift through me,
echoing in the empty places I don't know how to fill.
I've been clean long enough to know what I'm supposed to say.

I could stand, speak, tell them about the wreckage,
about the nights that almost swallowed me whole,
about the way I crawled my way back.

I could let their nods stitch me into the fabric of this room,
make myself belong.
But my throat stays tight, my hands stay still.
Not because I don't have a story,
but because I'm afraid they'll hear it and still not see me.

So I wait.

For something. For nothing. For a sign.
For the voice of Yahweh.
to press into my ribs and remind me I'm real.
For someone to turn, meet my gaze,
and understand without me having to explain.
But there is no divine revelation.
No voice breaking through the static.
Just the low hum of people breathing, shifting, moving,
just the steady, unremarkable proof that I am still here.

And maybe, for tonight, that is enough.

IV. Where the Ash Settles
Not Just Surviving; Becoming

This section is about what comes after—the slow, unsteady steps of rebuilding, the quiet weight of survival, and the moments where hope begins to feel real again. It doesn't claim that healing is easy or that grief ever fully fades. Instead, it sits in the space between—between loss and renewal, between absence and presence, between the past that still lingers and the future that is, somehow, still possible.

These poems don't pretend that sobriety erases pain or that time alone can mend what's broken. They acknowledge the empty chairs, the ghosts that still whisper, the silence that used to be unbearable. They honor the ones who didn't make it back while holding space for the ones who did. And most of all, they recognize that survival isn't just about not dying—it's about learning how to live again.

This is the part of the journey where the ash settles, where the weight starts to shift, where something small but steady hums beneath the wreckage. It doesn't promise an easy road, but it does promise this:

You are still here. And for now, that's enough.

The Noise That Comes After

I used to pray for peace.
Swore if I could just get clean,
just get through the fucking night
without shaking hands and a stomach tied in knots,
without the itch crawling under my skin,
I'd be okay.
But nobody told me about this part.
Nobody warned me that silence isn't soft.
It doesn't wrap around you like a warm fucking blanket.
It settles in your bones like a weight,
like a question you don't want to answer.
It presses into your ribs,
fills the spaces where chaos used to live,
where the high used to hum.
I used to know what to do with my hands.
A bottle, a lighter, a rig, a tooter—
something to hold, something to chase.
Now they just hover in my lap,
useless, restless,
fingers twitching against nothing.
I sit in my bedroom,
under the comfiest duvet,
no music, no voices, no hum of a TV
to drown out the sound of my own thoughts.
I didn't know they could be this loud.
Didn't know they could circle like vultures,
picking at the past, at the parts of me
I thought I buried.
I close my eyes,
but the silence stays.
No static. No escape hatch.
Just me, still breathing.
Just me, still here.
And fuck, maybe that's something.
Maybe one day, I'll get used to it.
Maybe one day, the quiet won't feel like a goddamn threat.
But tonight, it's heavy.
Tonight, I sit with it.
Tonight, I don't run.

The Long Way Back

Nearly twelve years.
Twelve fucking years,
and here I am, sitting in these chairs
with only eighty-five days to my name.
A newcomer, again.

The same goddamn script,
the same stale coffee,
the same fluorescent lights buzzing like a goddamn joke.
I used to be the one giving advice,
talking about willingness, about grace,
about how I stayed clean no matter what.

I used to nod at the newcomers,
tell them it gets easier,
tell them to keep coming back.
And now I'm the one
counting my days like a kid learning numbers,
like they mean something,
like they might hold me together
before I slip through the cracks again.

I don't know how I got here.
Or maybe I do.

Maybe it was the slow unravel,
the meetings I stopped going to,
the phone calls I left unanswered,
the voice in my head that whispered,
"You've got this now. You're different.
You don't need them anymore."
And for a while, I believed it.
For a while, I thought I was free.

But the thing about this disease?
It doesn't scream—it waits.
It sits patient as a vulture,
watching for the moment you get tired,
the moment you let your guard down,
the moment you think you're safe.
And then it pulls you back under.

So here I am, eighty-five days clean,
hands shaking as I countdown to that red keytag,
"I'm an addict... again."
The words taste like rust in my mouth.

Like shame. Like regret.
Like everything I swore I'd never feel again.
I hate it. I fucking hate it.

But I keep showing up.
I keep sitting in these chairs.
I keep counting these goddamn days,
because the only thing worse
than starting over
is not making it back at all.
And I know that story all too well.

Letters to the Ones I Lost

The grease from the fryers stuck to my skin,
wings burning under the heat lamps,
orders stacking up like we'd never dig our way out.
Lenny leaned against the counter,
grinning like the whole damn restaurant
was some inside joke only he got.
"You're killing it, beast,"
he'd say, tossing a rag over his shoulder,
sneaking fries when the managers weren't looking.
We ran on stolen sips of Monster and smoke breaks,
on the belief that life was long
and there'd always be another shift.
I quit that job years ago,
but some nights, I still feel the rush of it,
still hear him laughing over the chaos,
like he's just in the next room,
like I could turn the corner and find him there.

Julie had this way of making everything feel safe.
Game of Thrones nights on our couch,
wrapped in blankets like winter really was coming,
predicting deaths like we had any control.
She'd roll her eyes at me, throw popcorn,
tell me to shut the fuck up and just watch.
We swore we'd finish the series together,
but the last season came and went,
and I couldn't bring myself to hit play without her.
The show ended, but she's still frozen in time,
still mid-sentence, still alive
in a world where Ned Stark never loses his head,
where the story never has to end.

Jimmy was all motion—
Six Flags in the dead heat of summer,
long lines, sticky asphalt,
him hyping up the next ride
like it was life or death.
We rode every coaster twice,
drunk on adrenaline and bad decisions,
chasing the kind of high
we didn't have to pay for.
It felt infinite,
the wind in our faces, the world rushing by,
but we were always headed toward the drop.
I still drive past that exit sometimes,
still hear his voice daring me

to go faster, go higher,
like the fall was never something to be afraid of.

I don't know why I'm still here and you're not.
Why my lungs still fill and yours don't.
Why I still get to wake up, drink my coffee,
watch the reruns, hear the next inside joke,
ride another goddamn rollercoaster.
But I carry you.
In the hum of a busy kitchen,
in the glow of a TV screen,
in the rush of wind and the pull of gravity.
I carry you, even when it hurts.
Even when I wish I didn't have to.

V. Between Ruin and Revelation
The Places That Carry Us Forward

This section is about the spaces that hold us when we are rebuilding—whether it's a crowded sober living house, a dimly lit meeting hall, a Zoom room full of old-timers fumbling with mute buttons, or the pulse of music on a dance floor where no one needs a drink to belong. It's about trying again, about sitting in the loneliness that lingers even in rooms filled with people, about learning to exist in the quiet after years of chaos. It's about the places where healing doesn't come easy, where survival isn't pretty, where connection feels like a risk, but we take it anyway.

These poems live in the tension between isolation and community, between wanting to disappear and choosing to stay. They are about the nights spent pressed against city lights, screaming along to songs that remind us we are still alive. They are about hands reaching through screens when the world shut down, about making a home in the unexpected, about finding meaning in rituals both sacred and mundane.

This is what comes after the breaking—where the past still haunts, but the future begins to whisper. It is not a perfect return. It is not a clean slate. But it is something. And for now, for today, that is enough.

The Second First Time

Sober living, round two.
Not a fresh start—just another attempt.
December's wreckage still clings to my ribs,
but it's winter now,
and I am here, trying again.
Forty of us crammed into Pashek Headquarters,
elbows knocking, cards slapping against the table,
voices sharp with laughter, with arguments,
with inside jokes that weren't mine before,
but might be now.
The house smells like burnt coffee and microwave dinners,
like too many bodies in one space,
like something I almost trust.
I still wake up some mornings
with my bones aching for things I can't have,
but Friday nights come,
and the craving dulls beneath the weight of this—
this ridiculous, chaotic mess
of recovering addicts talking shit over Mafia,
of someone always standing in the kitchen
trying to fix a chair that's been broken for weeks.
I let it hold me.
I let it be enough.
And when the weekend rolls in,
I pull on my black boots,
line my eyes dark,
and head downtown to the club.
Not for shots.
Not for anything except the music,
the pulse of it shaking my ribs,
the way my body remembers how to move
without needing a drink to loosen the edges.
Emo night.
The songs of my youth howling through the speakers,
every lyric still buried under my skin.
I scream the words with strangers,
with friends,
with people who knew the same kind of darkness
and still chose to dance.
And for a moment, I forget.
Forget that I am rebuilding,
that I almost didn't make it back,
that I still don't know what the fuck I'm doing.
I let the bass shake the doubt out of my chest,
let the cold night air bite my skin
as I step outside between songs,

My lungs craving a smoke.
I am here.
I am breathing.
I am standing in the city lights,
lungs full of winter,
alive in a way I never thought I'd be again.

Scales Fell Like Rain

Christianity fit like a wet glove—
clinging, heavy, shapeless,
molded to hands that never truly felt like mine.
It was all I had ever known.
The hymns, the prayers, the promises,
a gilded chain, a weight they called a gift,
dragging behind me like a shadow I wasn't allowed to leave.
I wore it because I was told to.
Because faith was inheritance.
Because questioning was rebellion.
Because the hands that fed me also folded in prayer,
and so I folded mine too.
But it never kept me warm.
So I never questioned.
The Faith began to comfort—
until it didn't.
Until I sat in the passenger seat of Leslie's SUV,
rain streaking the windows,
her car polished to a mirror sheen,
a perfect reflection of the woman she presented to the world—
polished, practiced, put-together.
Between us, my fifth fifth step,
it lay open between us,
pages spread like the wreckage of a life I barely survived.
Every fear, every failure, every truth
I had tried to drown, now written in ink,
no longer able to be ignored.
And as we read, the scales fell from my eyes.
It wasn't dramatic—no flash of light,
no burning bush, no voice from the heavens.
Just silence:
there was no Satan.
Hell did not exist.
There was no great punishment waiting
for the moments I stepped out of line.
No eternal damnation for the thoughts I couldn't control.
There was nothing looming over me,
nothing waiting to strike me down.
Just the weight of a fear
that had never been mine to carry. Just a belief that was never mine to hold.
I looked at Leslie. She nodded.
Didn't try to fix it, didn't try to pull me back in.
Just let me sit there, listening to the rain,
watching my faith loosen,
softening like ink on wet paper.

**And for the first time,
I was not afraid.**

When the Gods Found Me

I did not find them in the beginning.
I did not call them by name.
Did not know their voices,
did not know how to pray
to anything that wasn't watching,
judging, waiting for me to fail.
The tarot cards came first—
hands trembling, shuffling,
asking questions I wasn't brave enough to say out loud.
I flipped cards like scripture,
searching for something, anything,
that didn't demand my guilt
before it offered me grace.
Hekate lit the path.
Maiden, Mother, and Crone wove the threads.
Not saviors, not rulers—guides.
They did not promise salvation,
did not ask for my knees on the ground,
only for my feet in the dirt,
only for my voice in the wind.
And I walked with them,
until relapse came for me again.
Until I was empty and aching.
Until I had to start over.
But this time, I was not alone.
The Gods of the soil where I was raised
stood beside me,
held my shaking hands
through my second and third step.
Not a God above me,
but spirits beside me,
leading me forward one breath at a time.
Wodan called my name.
Frau Perchta sharpened my spine.
Not to silence my anger,
not to smother my rage,
but to teach me how to wield it.
How to hold wrath in my hands
without letting it burn me alive.
How to name my fury and walk through it,
as I tore my fourth step apart,
spilling ink like blood,
spitting truth like fire.
And then—the twelfth fifth step.
The last time I sat before my sponsor,
truth laid bare, voice steady,

rage softened into grief,
and Frau Holle wiped my tears.
This is how the Gods found me.
Not on my knees, begging.
Not in surrender.
But standing, walking, breaking, healing.
And they never once asked me
to be anything other than what I am.
They only asked me to keep going.

The Weight of Me

I was six when I screamed at Yahweh,
my voice raw with rage,
a child's fists clenched against an unseen sky.
Why me? Why me?
I wanted to be anyone but myself,
a shadow cast in someone else's light,
a name unspoken, a soul untouched.

Now, at thirty-three, I call to Wodan,
the same cry, the same hollow ache,
wrapped in years of knowing
that the answers don't come in echoes.
Still, I demand them.

I rage at the life I have been given,
at the sharp edges that carve into my skin,
at the way my mind splits the world in two—
black or white, right or ruin,
never a middle path to stand upon.

But I am learning.
I am learning to see the triggers before they spark,
to name the storms before they break.
I will step into treatment,
walk through the doors of the center
and ask—no, beg—for guidance,
for something to soften this jagged thinking,
to quiet the hands that have tried to silence me.

I have learned that an addict alone
is in bad company.
That isolation is a wound that festers,
a whisper that becomes a scream.
That those of us who seek recovery
must embrace surrender, humility, and faith.
And I am trying.
I am trying to hold those things close,
even when my hands tremble.

My attitude has been a weapon turned inward,
a knife I have learned too well.
But I want to turn it around.
I want to believe that I am more
than my scars and my sorrow.

So, I will take this step,

not because I feel strong,
but because I know I am breaking.
And in the breaking,
maybe—just maybe—
there is room to heal.

Between Hoofbeats and Whispers

This morning, I wake with the Buffalo.
Steady. Rooted. Whole.
The Sacred Hoop feels unbroken,
and I walk in balance,
carrying the wisdom of the four directions,
feet firm upon Grandmother Earth.
I breathe deep—today, I am strong.
The trees nod as I pass,
the wind hums an old song,
and the world does not feel so heavy.
For a moment, I believe I belong.

But I know what comes next.
By evening, I become the Mouse.
Small. Darting. Overwhelmed.
I scurry through the undergrowth of my thoughts,
nose twitching, heart racing,
seeing everything, yet understanding nothing.
Every worry, a seed I gather,
hoarding my fears in hidden places.

The Sacred Hoop frays at the edges,
and I forget the lessons of the Elders.
I feel cut off from the Circle,
from the teachings, from the Medicine.
The weight settles behind my ribs,
my mind restless, my spirit uncentered.

I whisper to myself:
Tomorrow, I will seek the Buffalo again.
Tomorrow, I will walk in balance.
Tomorrow, I will trust the Wisdom Keepers,
listen for the voices in the wind,
and let the drum of my heart guide me home.

Because healing is not a straight path.
It is the cycle of night and day,
of Buffalo and Mouse,
of falling and rising,
of remembering, again and again,
that I am still here.

The Way Home

It came quiet, like a song hummed under breath,
like light spilling through the cracks of an old, boarded-up house.
I almost didn't trust it—
sat there, waiting for the weight to settle,
for the shadow to creep back in.
But it didn't.
It was winter, the kind that sinks into the bones,
where the cold stretches wide, endless,
where my body ached in ways I didn't have words for.
Pain had become my shadow,
my skin a battleground of exhaustion,
each movement a war I never wanted to fight.
But then—The Way Home.
A show, just a show, I told myself,
but somehow, it was an anchor,
something to tether me
when my body felt like it was unraveling.
I sat with my mom, miles apart,
thirteen hours of road between us,
but still, we watched together.
Still, we held onto the same story.
Still, we pressed play at the same time,
her voice on the phone, warm, steady,
wrapping around me like a blanket I couldn't touch.
The pain didn't go away,
but for an hour at a time,
it didn't win.
For an hour at a time,
I wasn't just my body screaming,
wasn't just waiting for the next wave of hurt.
For an hour at a time,
I was a daughter,
I was here,
I was something other than surviving.
And maybe that's what joy is—
not loud, not overwhelming,
but something that slips in through the cracks,
something that lingers between the ache,
something that stays, even when the pain does.
And I thought—
Maybe this time, it stays.

This Time, I Breathe

I don't know when it changed.
When the weight didn't feel like an anchor,
when the quiet stopped sounding like a threat.
Maybe it didn't happen all at once.
Maybe it never does.
But somewhere in the middle of another meeting,
another long drive home,
another morning where I actually got out of bed,
I realized I wasn't waiting to disappear anymore.
The grief is still here—
it still lingers in the empty chairs,
in the names we whisper in remembrance,
in the songs that hit too hard on bad days.
But it's not drowning me.
Not anymore.
I drink my coffee,
hot and bitter, steam curling into the cold air.
I step outside, let the wind slap color into my cheeks,
watch the world move in ways I never used to notice.
There is something alive in the air today.
Something that hums beneath my skin,
not an ache, not an itch—
something quieter.
Something that stays.
I still miss them.
I still wonder why I made it back when they didn't.
But I keep going,
because that's the only way I know to honor them now.
By waking up.
By showing up.
By staying.
And maybe I won't always feel like this—
steady, sure, almost whole.
Maybe there are still dark days waiting for me.
But for now, the ash has settled.
For now, I am here.
And for the first time in a long time,
that's enough.

Muted, Unmuted, Still Here

At first, it felt like drowning.
The world went quiet, streets emptied, doors locked.
Meetings shut down, rooms once filled with coffee and laughter
became nothing but memory.
I sat in my grandma's double-wide, counting days
the way I used to count pills,
feeling the weight of silence press into my ribs.
The river had come again, pulling everything I knew downstream.
No more late-night parking lot talks,
no more hands clasped in prayer,
no more folding into a hug that said you are not alone.
I was alone.
But then—Zoom.
Not strangers, not faces I didn't know—
my home group, full of old-timers who still had flip phones,
who swore up and down they'd never touch a computer,
who grumbled at the idea of "online meetings"
like it was blasphemy.
And somehow, it became my job to get it running.
Every day, noon sharp.
My job to keep the meeting open,
to make sure they had somewhere to go.
Fifteen men and women with twenty-plus years in the program—
and me, barely three years clean,
the least qualified person in the room
somehow holding the key to keeping us together.
Every day, I sent out the link, opened the room,
waited for their names to pop up in tiny squares.
Listened to their voices crackle through bad connections,
watched them fumble with mute buttons,
saw their faces soften when the screen filled
with people they never thought they'd see again.
Their relief became mine.
The river took the world I knew,
but it gave me something new, something vast.
It carved a path I never would have chosen,
but one I could still walk.
I did not drown.
I did not sink.
I let the water carry away what no longer served me.
And when I stepped onto solid ground again,
I was not the same—
but I was still here.
Along with almost everyone else.

Fire, Earth, and Breath

I used to wake up empty,
rolling out of bed with nothing to say,
no prayers, no thanks, just another day
I wasn't sure I wanted.
I didn't believe in morning light,
not the way other people did,
not in the way it was supposed to be a promise.
But now, I wake with Kaakwha.
Golden light stretching over the horizon,
soft but certain,
her warmth pressing against my skin
before I even open my eyes.
She reminds me—
breathe, rise, begin.
I step outside, feet bare in the dirt,
pressing my palms into the earth.
Eagentci holds steady beneath me,
a heartbeat older than time,
reminding me that I am real,
that I belong to this place,
that I do not have to float away.
The cravings creep in as the night settles,
whispering old things in a voice I almost miss.
But Gagqa watches from the branches,
black feathers glinting under the moon.
He does not stop the hunger,
does not silence the ghosts—
but he teaches me how to see them
without letting them lead me home.
I make tea with Frau Holle in the steam,
in the warmth curling against my face,
in the patience of a slow sip.
She is the breath between pain,
the quiet hum of rest,
the knowing that healing is not a race
but something softer, something that stays.
Some days, the rage still burns,
a fire I have yet to learn to control.
Some days, I want to tear it all down,
to rip the seams of every injustice,
to let my own fury be the thing that remakes me.
Wodan and Frau Perchta sit with me in that fire.
They do not ask me to put it out.
They remind me that rage is a forge,
that destruction is only one side of the blade.
I light a candle. I whisper a name.

I press my palms into the dirt.
I walk into the day
with open hands.
As I dance,
And chant,
As the sun rises,
I give thanks to this beautiful life,
A life I fought long and hard for.

VI. Waking the Bones

Prayers in the Ash

This section stands at the meeting place of survival and sacredness, where the fight for sobriety is intertwined with something older, something deeper. It is where gods and spirits walk alongside the wounded, where rage is not something to smother, but something to forge. It is where healing is not passive—it is an act of will, a call to power, a choice made over and over again.

Here, Hekate stands at the crossroads, her torch flickering not with easy answers but with the promise that the path must be chosen, not given. Frau Holle, mother of winter's hush and the spindle's weave, reminds us that time moves in cycles—pain is never permanent, but neither is comfort. Wodan and Frau Perchta take rage in their hands, not to erase it, but to shape it into something sharp and steady, something that cuts away the rot without destroying the root.

This is where the gods are not distant. They are in the dirt beneath our palms, the wind that hums through bare trees, the light stretching over the horizon. Kaakwha, the first breath of dawn, reminds us that truth does not always arrive in a roar—sometimes, it is in the quiet persistence of rising again. Eagentci steadies shaky hands, pressing feet firm against the earth, whispering that we are still here. And Gagqa, dark-feathered and watchful, does not banish the past but teaches us how to sit with it without losing ourselves.

There is no promise of ease here. There is no god offering to take away the weight entirely. But there is power—power in choosing the path forward, power in using rage as a blade rather than a wrecking ball, power in knowing that between light and shadow, between strength and struggle, we are not walking alone.

Between Hoofbeats and Currents

Some mornings, I wake up with the strength of the white buffalo.
Feet firm against the earth, breath steady,
a heartbeat that doesn't waver.
The world opens its arms to me—
trees nodding in the breeze, rivers humming their quiet songs.
I move through it like I belong, like I was made for this,
hooves pounding, earth trembling,
carried by something rare, something ancient.
I don't falter. I don't doubt.
I am steady. I am whole.
But when the sun sinks and the sky folds into itself,
I am no buffalo.
I am a salmon fighting the current,
water pressing in, heavy, unrelenting.
The river is sharp with unseen stones,
the cold wraps around my ribs,
and every inch forward feels like drowning.
I flail. I gasp.
I forget what steady even feels like.
Maybe this is how it goes—
buffalo in the morning, salmon at night.
Strong under the sun, struggling in the dark.
Both of them mine, both of them true.
So I let the day carry me forward,
and I let the river push against me.
And somewhere between hoofbeats and currents,
between rising and resisting,
I learn what it means to survive.

The Hex Unwoven

I wake with the Ten of Swords lodged in my back,
black blades slick with the ghosts of a thousand mistakes.
The crows still circle, wings stretched like shadows,
waiting for me to stay down, to give in, to rot.
I have worn this ruin too long,
let it stitch itself into my ribs,
let it name me as something already buried.
Not today.
I light the candle, strike the match with shaking hands.
Smoke curls up, thick as memory,
thick as the lies I once let coil around my throat.
The Devil grins from the table, his hooves planted firm,
his tangled cords wrapping tight,
whispering that I will never be free.
I press my thumb against the flame
until the skin stings, until the voice fades,
until the bindings blacken and burn.
The hex unwinds, thread by thread.
Reiki hums in my palms, heat spilling from my fingers
as I trace the wounds I once tried to carve out of myself.
The past flickers, tries to stay,
but I let it pass through me—
a serpent shedding skin, a candle melting down to nothing.
I call my energy back,
from the hands of lovers who never held me right,
from the mouths of those who only spoke in poison.
I pull my name from their tongues,
sever the tie, cut the cord clean.
The Tower still looms in my chest,
jagged and waiting for the next strike of lightning,
but I am not afraid of falling anymore.
I am fireproof now.
The ground may shake, the bricks may crumble,
but I do not.
I step into the circle,
salt at my feet, steel at my wrist,
the Mother of Wands coiled inside my chest—
serpent-backed and unbothered,
watching the flames rise without fear.
I hold the match, I hold the blade,
I hold myself for the first time in years.
The hex is broken.
The spell is mine now.
And this time, I do the naming.

Between Light and Shadow

Kaakwha, Morning Flame, Keeper of Truth—
You are the first breath of dawn,
the golden thread stitching the sky to the earth.
Let your light pour into my hollow places,
fill the cracks that addiction left behind.
Burn away the lies I once told myself,
the ones that whispered I was beyond saving.
Let me wake and rise with you,
not just to exist, but to begin again.

Eagentci, Steady Earth, Mother of All—
Hold me when I shake, when I stumble,
when the past claws at my ribs.
Let my hands press into your soil,
let my feet sink into your strength.
Remind me that I am not weightless,
not something meant to drift and disappear.
I belong here, among the roots,
where things break and bloom and grow again.

Gagqa, Night-Winged Watcher, Keeper of Secrets—
You see what lurks in the dark,
the old hunger, the ghosts I have named.
You do not banish them—you do not need to.
Instead, you teach me how to see,
how to stand in the night without losing myself.
Let me hear your call in the quiet,
a reminder that I am still here, still breathing,
that I can hold my past without drowning in it.

Between light and shadow, between earth and sky,
I walk forward.
Not alone. Not lost.
But carried, rooted, guided.

Hekate's Crossroads

The road splits in three,
dirt packed down by the weight of every step before mine.
I stand at the edge, breath heavy in my chest,
smoke curling from the wick of an unlit candle.
I do not move.
Not yet.
The trees here are old—older than memory, older than prayer.
Their roots press deep, twisting beneath the soil,
whispering in a language I almost understand.
The wind shifts, carrying something colder, something known.
She is here.
Hekate waits where the shadows stretch long.
No words, just the steady burn of her torch,
just the flicker of something ancient in her gaze.
She does not tell me where to go.
She does not promise I will make it through.
She only holds the flame, steady, unwavering,
and I am the one who has to choose.
The road behind me is littered with ghosts,
every misstep, every relapse, every night I begged for an exit.
I could turn back, but I won't.
Not this time.
The Maiden hums in the rustle of the leaves,
young, wild, daring me to step forward.
The Mother watches in the flickering torchlight,
warm and sharp, patient and unyielding.
The Crone lingers in the hush of the dark,
her silence carrying every lesson I am still afraid to learn.
I kneel at the crossroads, fingers digging into the dirt.
The earth hums beneath my palms, steady, waiting.
I press my forehead to the ground and offer what I have—
a breath, a whisper, the last of my fear.
And when I rise, I choose.
One step, then another.
The torch still burns, even when I no longer see it.
Even when the path is unknown.

By Silver Thread and Spindle's Weave

Through the frost-laced air, through the hush before the storm.
You who shake the down from heaven's pillows,
who weave the wind into lullabies and warnings,
who pull the thread of what was and what will be.
I am tired, hands trembling against the weight of another night.
The fever clings, the ache settles deep,
bones heavy, breath thin, skin too tight.
I do not ask for the pain to leave—
only that I do not break beneath it.
Wrap me in your wool-thick warmth,
your quiet patience, your winter silence.
Hold me steady as the seasons shift,
as the last brittle leaves fall and the earth turns inward.
Let me rise when it is time.
By silver thread and spindle's weave,
stitch me back into myself.
Not untouched, not unscarred,
but whole enough to walk forward.
Whole enough to stay.

Forge My Fury

Wodan, storm-bringer, battle-born,
your name runs wild in the howl of the wind,
in the sharp crack of thunder against the earth.
You wield the spear, the poet's tongue,
the fire that burns and the wisdom that stays.
I do not ask for mercy.
I ask for sight—
to see my rage for what it is,
to wield it like a blade, not a wrecking ball,
to let it carve, to let it cleanse,
to let it leave something standing when the fire dies down.

Frau Perchta, keeper of the blade,
you who spin fate with one hand
and sever with the other—
teach me the weight of what should be cut
and what must remain.
My anger is sharp, wild, restless.
I do not want it dulled.
I want it shaped.
Temper it, grind it down to something true,
let it cut away the rot, but never the root.
Let me stand in the wreckage without becoming it.

Wodan, Perchta, gods of fire and reckoning,
do not take this rage from me.
Turn it to steel, not rust.
Let my hands be craft, my voice be flame,
my soul unbroken, my name still mine.
With the breath of wolves and the will of oak,
I walk into this fire.
Let me rise from it,
not burned, not hollow—
but whole.

Hallowed Ground

Persephone stares back at me in the mirror,
her face too much like mine.
Not just in the cheekbones, the curve of the mouth,
but in the way she lingers—
caught between worlds, belonging to both,
belonging to neither.
I braid flowers into crowns,
lay them down like offerings,
watch the petals fold into the dirt,
their roots tangled in something older than memory.
The seasons turn like whispered spells,
like dice thrown in the dark,
like a promise I never agreed to but still have to keep.
I am the color in the shadows,
a flicker in the in-between.
Autumn's breath pulls me under,
but spring loosens its grip, just enough.
I ache with the rhythm of the wheel,
stitched into the fabric of longing,
woven tight between the living and the dead.
You are bound beneath the earth,
but I still reach for you,
fingers brushing the veil,
hoping that even now, you reach back.
Even time cannot unmake us.
Even fate cannot untangle this thread.
So let the seasons shift,
let the story keep spinning.
I have walked through both worlds,
and I know now—
this love does not die.

VII. In Closing

The Cold Unknown

In the cold unknown, where waters seep,
Ebb and flow, a solemn journey deep.
Away from me, pain's transient woes,
Mud between my toes, where darkness grows.

A flame that burns, its smoke adrift,
The water's turn, a silent, subtle gift.
A lover's kiss, a dance in the air,
A pentacle crossed, a maiden fair.

A note tossed, love's words spoken true,
Prayers of a mother, how about you?
To the Gods, I pray for life's blessing,
Devil's law, a strife confessing.

For hope, I plead, how about you?
A lowered rope, an unexpected cue.
Around my neck, the rope entwines,
No hope remains, in shadowy confines.

Now I rest, as the echoes wane,
In the silence, a soul's final refrain.

Longing for the Forest

I grew up where the road was not a line,
but a story traced in dust and ruts,
woven by tires and boots and hooves,
its edges frayed by grasses and wildflowers,
its voice a low murmur of crunch and give
beneath my wandering feet.
Mornings smelled of dew-soaked earth,
the sky blushed pale as the waking sun,
and sparrows wove songs through the air,
their notes caught in the gnarled arms of oaks.
At dusk, the crickets played a hymn
as shadows draped the hills in peace.
My hands remember the warmth of the soil,
the way it would yield and hold,
carrying the rhythm of life unseen—
roots, worms, the sigh of rain-soft clay.
Every step on that road was a prayer,
a quiet devotion to the wild.
But life beckoned me to the city's hum,
to towers that scrape the clouds,
where the streets pulse with ceaseless motion
and the air is thick with exhaust and ambition.
I traded the dirt road's lullaby
for the rush of trains and neon's glare.
Yet my heart aches for the soft curves
of that road, for the way it disappeared
into the horizon with no promises,
no urgency, no end.
I miss the stars that dared to shine,
unhidden by the city's ceaseless glow,
and the silence that wrapped itself around me
like the familiar arms of an old friend.
In dreams, I wander back,
to that place where the wind carries no urgency,
where the road whispers my name
in the language of dust and memory,
and the earth remembers my steps
long after I've passed.

A Garland of Blossoms

A wild daisy, simple and bright,
Its petals pale as morning's light,
Spins and sways in the summer's breath,
A fleeting joy on the twilight's crest.
A tulip blooms with a blush of rose,
Where soft winds whisper and rivers flow.
Petals bow in their gentle flight,
A toast to beauty in the fading light.
A rose of crimson, bold and rare,
Climbs my gate with tender care.
Its blossoms speak of friendship's grace,
A fleeting kiss, a soft embrace.
The dahlia stirs in golden hue,
A radiant gem in morning's dew.
She lifts her face, her beauty clear,
And I am stilled, my heart sincere.
The lily rests, a fragrance sweet,
Wound in a wreath where spirits meet.
Perhaps this bloom is love's first taste,
Her kiss upon my lips, a grace.
An orchid's bloom beneath the sun,
Softly glowing, her heart undone.
Her gaze meets mine, and time stands still,
Two souls entwined, one shared will.

Kiera J. Gerety has been part of the recovery community since April 25, 2013. She knows the quiet devastation of a few-day relapse and the heavy, aching attempt of pretending to be "normal" for a year. Some of her loneliest times were spent deep in recovery service—and yet, being of service to the recovery community has given her the biggest sense of freedom. From working for conferences designed for and by young people in recovery to chairing a literature committee, these times have truly shaped her.

Kiera attended college at Waynesburg University and the University of Massachusetts, Dartmouth.

She was born and raised in Brown Hill, a wooded pocket of Cambridge Springs, Pennsylvania, where she found a sense of community with those commiserating with her on the school bus. Her adult years led her to Pittsburgh, where she worked as a waitress and a bartender. Outside of writing, she finds joy in the worlds of Dungeons & Dragons and gaming, where her imagination truly runs wild.

Kiera extends her deepest gratitude to Nichole, Sharlee, Kate, Alysha, and Morgan—the women in whose presence she never felt loneliness.

She now lives in Kansas City with her wife and a household full of spirited cats and dogs who keep life messy, noisy, and full of love.

www.ingramcontent.com/pod-product-compliance
Lightning Source LLC
Chambersburg PA
CBHW022121090426
42743CB00008B/949